ALASKA'S NATIONAL LANDS

NORTH TO ALASKA

Lynn M. Stone

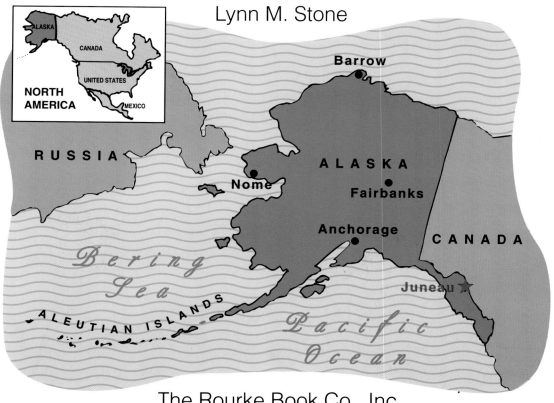

The Rourke Book Co., Inc.
Vero Beach, Florida 32964

Edited by Sandra A. Robinson

PHOTO CREDITS
Courtesy of Alaska Division of Tourism: pages 7 (Rex Melton), 10
(Robert Angell), 21; courtesy of National Park Service: page 15
(John Kauffmann); © Lynn M. Stone: cover, title page, pages 4, 8,
12, 13, 17, 18

Library of Congress Cataloging-in-Publication Data

Stone, Lynn M.
   Alaska's national lands / by Lynn M. Stone.
   p. cm. — (North to Alaska)
   Includes index.
   ISBN 1-55916-024-1
   1. National parks and reserves—Alaska—Juvenile literature.
2. Alaska—Description and travel—Juvenile literature. 3. Natural
history—Alaska—Juvenile literature. [1. National parks and
reserves. 2. Alaska—Description and travel. 3. Zoology—Alaska.]
I. Title. II. Series: Stone, Lynn M.   North to Alaska.
F905.S87 1994
917.98—dc20   93-43982
                                                             CIP
                                                              AC

c .001

TABLE OF CONTENTS

ALASKA'S NATIONAL LANDS

The United States government has saved some of Alaska's most beautiful and important places for all Americans to enjoy.

These lands and waters are Alaska's parks, forests, **preserves,** rivers, monuments and wildlife **refuges.** Most of these areas are kept natural and unspoiled.

Alaska's national lands have forests, mountains, lakes, volcanoes, plains, seashores and islands. They protect hundreds of kinds of fish, birds and mammals.

Alaska's national lands, owned by the American public, are homes for wolves and other wild animals

GLACIER BAY NATIONAL PARK

Visitors enter Glacier Bay National Park's wonderful world of water and ice by boat or float plane. The park has no roads.

Huge rivers of ice called **glaciers** meet the sea at Glacier Bay. Chunks of glaciers break off into the sea and become floating icebergs.

The forests and islands of Glacier Bay are homes for eagles, sea birds, bears and many other wild animals.

A section of glacier plunges into Glacier Bay

KATMAI NATIONAL PARK

Katmai National Park is a **remote** land of mountains, valleys, glaciers, salmon-filled streams and sea islands. In 1912, a powerful volcano erupted there. It left 40 square miles of rock and ash known as The Valley of Ten Thousand Smokes.

The moonlike valley no longer smokes, and visitors travel into it. However, it is the park's brown bears and excellent salmon fishing that attract visitors the most. Bears and fishermen sometimes share the best streams.

A brown bear digs for clams on a beach in Katmai National Park

LAKE CLARK NATIONAL PARK

Lake Clark National Park is a short flight across Cook Inlet from Anchorage.

Lake Clark has no roads, but trails and wild rivers lure people who love adventure — hikers, fishermen, campers, bird watchers and photographers.

Lake Clark National Park preserves a wilderness of mountains, woodland and water. Big-horned Dall sheep roam the mountain meadows. Brown bears, black bears, wolves and **caribou** also live in the park.

Snow-covered Mount Redoubt in Lake Clark National Park sends up a plume of volcanic smoke

An iceberg from Portage Glacier floats near the Portage Visitor Center in Chugach National Forest

*The far northern cousin of deer, caribou range
throughout the public lands of Alaska*

GATES OF THE ARCTIC NATIONAL PARK

Gates of the Arctic National Park is a huge wilderness in northern Alaska. The sharp peaks of the Brooks Range mountains rise above the park's deep valleys and rolling plains.

This is the second largest national park in the world. Only Wrangell-St. Elias National Park in Southeast Alaska is larger.

Huge herds of caribou live in Gates of the Arctic along with Dall sheep, wolverines, wolves, **lynxes,** eagles and falcons.

Anaktuvuk Pass is an Eskimo village within the park.

An Arctic stream rushes below the Arrigetch peaks in Gates of the Arctic National Park

DENALI NATIONAL PARK

Lying between Anchorage and Fairbanks, Denali is the easiest national park in Alaska to reach. Thousands of visitors drive or take the train to Denali each summer. From the park road visitors often see grizzlies, Dall sheep, moose and caribou.

On clear days, visitors gaze at snow-faced Mount McKinley. The mountain rises 20,320 feet above **sea level.** It is the highest peak in North America.

Autumn comes to the tundra below
Mount McKinley in Denali National Park

KENAI FJORDS NATIONAL PARK

Visitors to Kenai Fjords National Park near Seward travel by boat into Alaskan fjords (FYORDS). Fjords are narrow sea passages between mountain slopes or cliffs.

Kenai Fjords has glaciers, mountains, forests and several kinds of wild birds and mammals. Visitors enjoy watching mountain goats on the slopes and sea otters in the fjords.

A sea otter with her pup aboard paddles in Kenai Fjords National Park

TONGASS NATIONAL FOREST

America's national forests are more than woodlands. For example, the Tongass National Forest in Southeast Alaska has mountains, lakes, rivers, seashores and meadows. It also has the Mendenhall Glacier, a favorite visitor attraction.

The Tongass is home for bears, moose, deer, bald eagles, trumpeter swans, wolves, killer whales, trout and salmon.

Several million acres of the Tongass are "wilderness areas." They will stay roadless and wild.

A helicopter brings tourists to Mendenhall Glacier in the Tongass National Forest

CHUGACH NATIONAL FOREST

Like other national forests, the Chugach National Forest is a land of many uses. Logging is allowed in part of the Chugach. Other sections have been set aside by the U.S. Forest Service as wilderness areas.

People hike, camp, fish, boat and study nature in the Chugach. The forest has a visitor center about 50 miles south of Anchorage. There visitors can hike near Portage Glacier and a lake of icebergs.

Glossary

caribou (KARE uh boo) — large, northern cousins of deer, found in large herds; wild reindeer

glacier (GLAY shur) — a massive river of ice

lynx (LINKS) — a thick-furred wildcat of the Far North; the lynx resembles a bobcat

preserve (pre ZERV) — an area overseen by the U.S. Park Service and protected for certain natural resources, such as water

refuge (REH fewj) — a safe place; an area overseen by the U.S. Fish and Wildlife Service for the protection of certain wild animals

remote (re MOTE) — somewhere far away or out-of-the-way

sea level (SEE LEHV uhl) — the same height, or level, as the sea

INDEX